THE LIFE THAT NO ONE TAUGHT ME

D SUIAM

To my brother,

who supported me in doing the things I love to do.

And to all my readers who give their valuable time to read this book.

Contents

Inspiration Note

There is a story behind every poem in this collection, which is motivated by distinct counterparts of life. My sexuality and my past have played a crucial role in this collection. Also, the society that I live in without them tormented me. I won't possibly have my great creative thoughts such as this.

About The Author

D Suiam was Born and raised in Jaintia hills, Meghalaya, in the winter of 1999.

As a boy in his early childhood, the poet finds it difficult to figure out why he is so-called different from other boys when all he was doing was being himself. He spent most of his time in the school library, reading and started writing when he was in 9th grade. The author also has an interest in travelling around places and coffee sipping.

D Suiam has never published any book before but has written many articles for the social welfare LGBT+ community and the literature community.

Acknowledgements

I would like to express my thanks to Shyam Sunder for helping me make the right decision, for pushing me through the hard and soft of time and for being my very first reader of this collection and for providing insight into every step of it, for all those conversations in discussing to try and make this book more connected to the readers.

I can't thank my family and friends enough, especially my elder brother Wanmirang Suiam for believing in me and never letting me get out of their sight on this whole journey. Without their support, I would have lost in my own breath.

I would especially like to thank Bhamini Shree and the entire Mobbera Foundation for walking with me through this journey. You gave me hope and helped me realise that some dreams have come true when you have the right people around you.

Finally, but not least, I would like to extend my big thanks to all the readers out there who make time to read this book, for making it worth all the hard work and time that are putting into turning these collections of uncooked thoughts into a beautiful book.

Garden what I See

Oh! Beautiful garden

Trifling proportion,

Beautiful flowers around you

What an art I can sec

Inside you, the living

Oh countlessly alluring

Oh! beautiful garden

The world around me

With so much of Colours

Take a look and I see,

I can keep staring

Or take a walk across you

Oh! how dazzling just how I need you

Oh! Beautiful garden

From one place, I can see

With so much pleasure

Watching you leisurely

Oh! How fascinating

You just grow endlessly.

Bachelor season

The hot and the cold

The weather was so pink and mirthful

It's October and November yearly we get,

It's bachelor season, my mother said.

Oh! Nothing to bother about

It's just the season to get out

Where the falls are about to hit

With pleasure Air and nature are flourishes

The land with beautiful colours

Though it's loud, it sounds so peaceful

Oh! what a magical season

All the moments are abundant.

High school drama

Pink whether the season is four:

I started realising it when I was four.

Playinghood, mom I used to be;

Dad is someone that I wish to see,

but people around me make me feel crazy;

the high school drama as depressed as it could be:

Why can't you just stop and let me be me

Now I'm a man. I am sure of who I am

I'm still the same boy who doesn't have a plan,

Who eats the same food wakes up at the same time;

What you really say is not matter to me,

Because I know I'm gorgeous and exactly where I should be.

Just a child

I have been staring at the tree for so long that I almost know how it is growing,
But little did I know nutrition it's not the only thing that makes it keep going.

I don't know what I want, so please don't ask me.
Unless you want to be annoying because the only answer I have is "not even for me".

I'm just a child. Should I know what I'm doing?
Even though I'm 16th, no one taught me anything.
The only thing I know is that my schoolmate distressed my sexuality,
And the sole thing mater to my parent is this toxic society.

So should I be worry or just sip it like a coffee
Because no matter what's the struggle, if they can't follow what I do.
They would say, "I'm just a child". That can not be true.

It's not me, is you

we were the best we have,

there's nothing in this world you wouldn't laugh

until the day you realise who I am,

you say it's okay and nothing but calm

but the next I saw you,

it's nothing like I knew:

the question in my head never ended,

Am I something wrong, am I mistaken

stress start occurring until I realise,

it's not me is you who can't accept the truth,

it's all you who've changed and started being rude.

you judge things too fast,

which didn't last

You just shut me away,

just because I told you I‘m gay

I’m the same person, my dear

the only difference is back then, I hide,

Now I'm celebrating with Pride.

Calm down.

Living a life of pain and sorrow

I mask it up, worried about tomorrow

My life is miserable because of you, ignoramus

You put me down and make me think I'm bogus.

But I have learned the lesson of the stressing

People like you just love the discriminating

So just calm down as Taylor Swift say

Because nothing you say makes anyone less gay.

Do not think it much.

I met someone same as me

we share memories and become crazy

but that doesn't last long

nor anything went wrong

It's just guys like us who need to be left

you blame it on me while you're the one who kisses me

I just appreciate me you scared so much of society

you say you love me, but why leave me

after all, Love is Love isn't what you told me.

Now you're alone, isn't that what you want.

Or still, the same thing but the loss of someone

guess you just need not think much

because society is always going to judge.

Monsoon

Shss! What a day that rain wetted me.

The heated room with a cup of coffee

With a piece of slow music or just a lofi

Damn! They say it right home does feel cosy.

Monsoon is the season that I don't regret

After the heavy rain, the sunshine over my head

Sometimes the mist may cover up the day

But the wet ground beneath me is always there to stay.

It's not just me that felt calm and chilly

Even the nature was enjoying its frisky

Though sometimes we got teardown by storm

Still from it again, life does reform.

Debt

My elder told me I have to prepare for my future

But they never taught me how to be prepare

Everyone told me I needed money

But they never tell me if it grows on a tree

They tell me there are lots of free things you can get

But little did they know free things rouse to be in debt.

The debt that you can never be pay off

Because living just for you is already hard enough

Living it for someone isn't everyone's job.

22’

Here’s am 22

Strong enough but missing you

I don’t want to stay at home and cry

I just need my wings so I can fly

Because there’s so much outside my window

I just need a better view for me to go.

I don’t want to be 22 and worries

It’s time for my success stories.

Because the clock is ticking fastly

I need to get a dance at my forty.

Message To The Readers

"If you ever felt alone or left behind, remember that a pen and paper are just a minute away, and they are ready to listen to anything you got to say."

you can find me

email - davidsuiam29@gmail.com

Instagram - @d_suiam

9 798887 046624

Printed by Libri Plureos GmbH in Hamburg, Germany